# PENNSYLVANIA

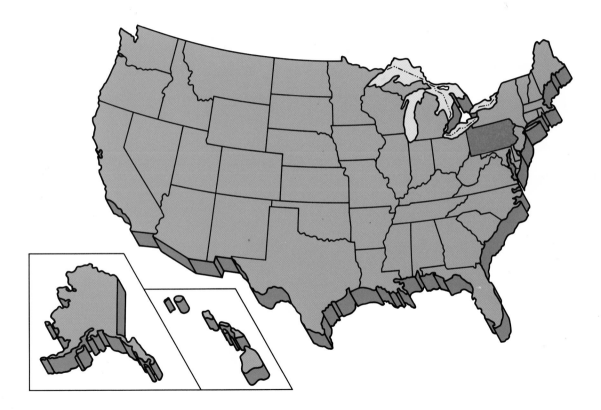

# PENNSYLVANIA

Gwenyth Swain

Lerner Publications Company

LIBRARY OF CONGRESS
CATALOGING-IN-PUBLICATION DATA
Swain, Gwenyth
    Pennsylvania / Gwenyth Swain.
      p. cm.—(Hello USA)
    Includes index.
    Summary: Introduces the history, geography, people, industries, and other highlights of Pennsylvania.
    ISBN 0-8225-2727-8 (lib. bdg.)
    1. Pennsylvania—Juvenile literature.
[1. Pennsylvania.] I. Title. II. Series.
F149.3.S93 1994
974.8—dc20              93-12333
                         CIP
                         AC

Manufactured in the United States of America

1  2  3  4  5  6  –  I/JR  –  99  98  97  96  95  94

Cover photograph—of a 100-year-old trolley in Pittsburgh—by James Blank/Root Resources.

The glossary that begins on page 68 gives definitions of words shown in **bold type** in the text.

 This book is printed on acid-free, recyclable paper.

# CONTENTS

PAGE  CHAPTER

**6   Did You Know . . . ?**
**9   A Trip Around the State**
**18  Pennsylvania's Story**
**43  Living and Working in Pennsylvania**
**55  Protecting the Environment**

SPECIAL SECTIONS

**40  *Historical Timeline***
**62  *Pennsylvania's Famous People***
**66  *Facts-at-a-Glance***
**68  *Pronunciation Guide, Glossary***
**70  *Index***

# Did You Know . . . ?

☐ America's most famous weather forecaster lives in Punxsutawney, Pennsylvania. On February second the Punxsutawney groundhog, known as Punxsutawney Phil, comes out of its hole. If the furry forecaster sees its shadow, six more weeks of winter are sure to follow. If the groundhog casts no shadow, spring is just around the corner.

Pittsburgh hasn't always been spelled with the letter *h* on the end. The *h* was added on permanently in the early 1900s.

Pennsylvania could be called the state of inventions. Hershey bars, Slinkys, steamboats, and banana splits all got their start in the state.

The Pennsylvania Dutch in southeastern Pennsylvania aren't Dutch at all. Their ancestors came from Germany and Switzerland in the late 1600s. They spoke German, or *Deutsch,* as it's called in German. Other settlers misunderstood and thought the newcomers were Dutch.

**Stone carvers finished Pittsburgh's main train station back when Pittsburgh was spelled without its final *h*.**

**Children** *(above)* **explore the mountains of northeastern Pennsylvania, while the turnpike** *(facing page)* **twists through mountains in the southwestern part of the state.**

# A Trip Around the State

If you want to travel around Pennsylvania, just hop on a highway. Pennsylvania is the place where big highways got their start. Back in 1940, travelers began driving on a section of Pennsylvania's **turnpike,** a four-lane toll road and the nation's first modern highway.

The turnpike crosses the state from east to west. This and other roads link Pennsylvania to its neighbors. Pennsylvania borders New York to the north, New Jersey to the east, Delaware and Maryland to the south, West Virginia to the southwest, and Ohio to the west.

**When seen from a hang glider high above, Pennsylvania's mountains look almost like hills.**

Mountains are the most important feature in the state's landscape. Pennsylvania's mountains are all part of the Appalachians, which began forming millions of years ago. From the mountains, the land slopes downward to rolling hills and lowlands.

Located in the middle of the Mid-Atlantic region of the United States, Pennsylvania has five major land regions. The Appalachian Plateau covers most of western and northern Pennsylvania. The region's broad-topped mountains, called plateaus, include the Allegheny and Pocono ranges of the Appalachian Mountains.

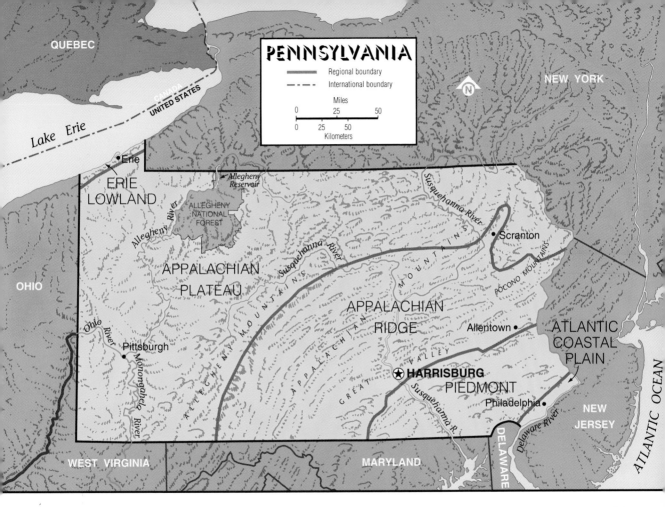

PENNSYLVANIA

Regional boundary

International boundary

Miles
0        25        50

0    25    50
Kilometers

N

QUEBEC

NEW YORK

Lake Erie

CANADA
UNITED STATES

Erie

ERIE LOWLAND

Allegheny Reservoir

ALLEGHENY NATIONAL FOREST

Susquehanna River

Scranton

POCONO MOUNTAINS

OHIO

Allegheny River

APPALACHIAN PLATEAU

Susquehanna River

MOUNTAINS

ALLEGHENY MOUNTAINS

APPALACHIAN RIDGE

Allentown

ATLANTIC COASTAL PLAIN

Ohio River

Pittsburgh

Monongahela River

APPALACHIAN MOUNTAINS

GREAT VALLEY

★ HARRISBURG

Susquehanna R.

PIEDMONT

Philadelphia

NEW JERSEY

ATLANTIC OCEAN

DELAWARE

Delaware River

WEST VIRGINIA

MARYLAND

11

Mountain ridges near Johnstown, in southwestern Pennsylvania, make for some hair-raising train rides.

The Appalachian Plateau holds a big share of the state's natural resources. The world's first successful oil well was drilled in the region in Titusville in 1859. Rich veins of coal have also been found and mined in the plateau region.

East of the Appalachian Plateau is the Appalachian Ridge, a region of steep, narrow mountain peaks and many valleys. Grouped together, a number of these valleys make up the Great Valley. Stretching from eastern Pennsylvania to the Maryland border, the Great Valley is famous for its fertile farmland.

**Farmland stretches across the Piedmont region.**

Farming is also important in the Piedmont region in southeastern Pennsylvania. The Piedmont's rolling land attracted many German and Swiss farmers, nicknamed the Pennsylvania Dutch, in the 1600s.

The northwestern tip of Pennsylvania borders Lake Erie.

Pennsylvania's smallest regions—the Atlantic Coastal Plain and the Erie Lowland—are both close to water. Part of a region that extends to the Atlantic Ocean, the coastal plain is a strip of lowland in the Delaware River valley.

The coastal plain is home to Philadelphia, the state's largest city and its first major port. Ships from Philadelphia reach the Atlantic Ocean by traveling south on the Delaware River.

In northwestern Pennsylvania, the Erie Lowland hugs the southern shore of Lake Erie, one of the **Great Lakes.** From the port city of Erie, Pennsylvania's products travel to other cities on the Great Lakes and beyond.

Most of Lake Erie is located outside Pennsylvania's borders. Inside the state are several large lakes, including the Allegheny Reservoir, an artificial lake in the Allegheny National Forest. Northeastern Pennsylvania is dotted with small lakes.

Rivers were the best travel routes in Pennsylvania before highways and turnpikes were built. Two of Pennsylvania's biggest rivers, the Allegheny and the Monongahela, join at Pittsburgh to form the Ohio River. The Susquehanna River meanders through the central part of the state, while the Delaware River marks Pennsylvania's eastern border.

**Hikers take a rest on a trail above the Susquehanna River near Harrisburg, Pennsylvania.**

Over half of Pennsylvania is covered with forest. Hickory, oak, and walnut trees thrive in southern Pennsylvania. Ruffed grouse, black bears, and muskrat live in the lush woods of northern Pennsylvania. Deer, raccoon, and rabbits are common throughout the state.

The Allegheny National Forest *(left)* on the Appalachian Plateau is home to ruffed grouse *(above)*, **bears** *(facing page)*, **and other animals.**

The state's climate and rainfall help trees and other plants grow. Pennsylvania averages 41 inches (104 centimeters) of rain and other **precipitation** each year.

Summers in Pennsylvania are warm, and winters are chilly but not bitterly cold. The average January temperature is 27° F (–3° C). In July temperatures rise to an average of 71° F (22° C).

From tree-covered mountain plateaus to rolling farmland to busy ports, Pennsylvania has a lot to offer. Whether you travel the turnpike or the back roads, the state is sure to surprise you.

# Pennsylvania's Story

People have lived in what is now Pennsylvania for over 12,000 years. About 15,000 American Indians were living in the area when Europeans first arrived in the 1600s. These Native Americans belonged to several different groups.

The Lenape made their homes in the broad valley of the Delaware River and were called Delawares by European settlers. The Susquehannocks, or "people of a well-watered land," lived along the Susquehanna River. The Monongahela lived in the west near the Ohio, Allegheny, and Monongahela rivers.

A Lenape Indian leader speaks to his people.

All of these groups lived mainly by farming. Corn, beans, and squash—all of which grew easily in river valleys—were major crops. Native Americans also harvested sap from maple trees.

To add to their diet and to provide skins for clothing, the Indians hunted deer, bears, and other animals. Fishing was also an important activity.

In 1609 British explorer Henry Hudson took a ship up the Delaware River and became the first European to meet the Lenape. Hudson worked for a Dutch fur-trading company.

Most of the Europeans who followed Hudson in the early 1600s were fur traders. In the 1630s, the Dutch set up trading posts near the Lenape on the western shores of the Delaware River. Swedish settlers soon followed. The Dutch and Swedes traded pots, guns, and cloth for furs from animals hunted by Native Americans.

By the 1640s, Dutch and Swedish settlers were arguing over control of the Delaware River valley. The Swedes had formed a **colony**, or settlement, called New Sweden near what is now Philadelphia.

In 1655 Dutch soldiers seized New Sweden. The struggle between the Dutch and the Swedes continued until 1664, when the British took control of the area.

People in Europe watched the settlers' progress with interest. William Penn of Great Britain thought the Delaware Valley would be a good place to live and farm.

Penn was a follower of George Fox. In the mid-1600s, Fox had started a religious movement called the Society of Friends, or Quakers. Friends believed in equality and in freedom to worship as they chose.

Swedish settlers in what became Pennsylvania maintained good relations with the Indians of the Delaware River valley.

21

William Penn was the founder of Pennsylvania, but the colony was named after his father. The ending *-sylvania* means "woods."

Penn dreamed of a new home where Friends and others could practice their religions freely. Pennsylvania was to be such a place.

On March 4, 1681, King Charles II of Britain gave Penn control of land west of the Delaware River. The king owed Penn's father a great deal of money. By granting land to William Penn, the king got rid of a large debt and a group of people he considered religious troublemakers.

Many Friends moved to the new colony of Pennsylvania, settling mainly in the Delaware Valley. German and Swiss people of the Amish and Mennonite faiths soon followed, attracted by good farmland and religious freedom. Scottish and Irish settlers also helped the colony's population grow.

Penn and other settlers got along well with their Native American neighbors. But as more Europeans arrived in the region, the Indians' homelands became smaller and more crowded.

**Quaker artist Edward Hicks imagined how a meeting between Penn and the Lenape might have looked.**

## Penn, the Lenape, and Peace

According to legend, Lenape leader Tamanend gave the wampum belt at left to William Penn in 1682 to celebrate a treaty, or agreement. The Lenape made wampum belts from strings of shell beads. The belts were considered sacred. Anyone holding a wampum belt was expected to tell the truth. On the belt given to Penn, two figures—one Lenape and one European—hold hands.

Penn and later colonists continued to meet with and buy land from Native Americans. Most of the land now known as Pennsylvania was purchased from the Indians by 1768. Over the years, more European settlers arrived and Pennsylvania's Indian population declined. Many Native Americans moved west, looking for better hunting grounds, while many others died from disease.

In 1754 the British and French argued over who would control North America. Many Native Americans joined forces with the French against the British in what became known as the French and Indian War.

Pennsylvania was a British colony, so most colonists sided with Great Britain. When the war ended,

JOIN, or DIE.

Made of segments standing for the British colonies, this cartoon snake was printed in the 1750s to urge colonists to stick together during the French and Indian War. It was used again 20 years later to unite the colonies against Great Britain.

the British had won control over large parts of North America, including all of what is now the state of Pennsylvania. The conflict, which lasted nearly 10 years, marked the end of peaceful relations between Indians and Europeans.

To pay for the war, Great Britain set high taxes on goods going to and from its colonies in North America. Many people in Pennsylvania and the other colonies were angered. They felt they were being treated unfairly.

25

**Independence Hall in Philadelphia was the site of the Second Continental Congress, the signing of the Declaration of Independence, and the writing of the U.S. Constitution.**

In 1774 representatives from the colonies gathered together in Philadelphia for a meeting they called the First Continental Congress. The colonists drew up a list of complaints against the British. They called for an end to unfair taxes and decided to stop trading with Great Britain.

British troops attacked the colonists in April 1775 to try to force them to stop their protests. At first it seemed that the two sides might reach a settlement. But when the Second Continental Congress met in Philadelphia in May, the colonies voted to fight for independence from Great Britain.

Legend has it that this was the bell that rang at Independence Hall on July 4, 1776. Since then, the Liberty Bell has become a symbol of freedom.

On July 4, 1776, about a year after the American War of Independence had begun, the Continental Congress passed the Declaration of Independence. In the declaration, 13 colonies officially claimed to be independent of Great Britain. They were forming a new, free country, whether the British liked it or not.

But the British did not intend to lose the colonies. In September 1777, at the Battle of Brandywine near Philadelphia, British redcoats surrounded the Continental Army, led by General George Washington. The British took Philadelphia, and the Continental Army was lucky to get out alive.

27

Washington and his soldiers were still smarting from their defeat when they settled in for the winter at Valley Forge, northwest of Philadelphia. Food soon ran short. Then smallpox broke out. Some of the men deserted and others died, but the Continental Army held together. The long, hard winter made the soldiers even more determined to fight on.

During the war, Pennsylvania's farmers grew grain to feed soldiers and horses. American troops, including many from Pennsylvania, used gunpowder from the colony's factories.

By the time the colonists had defeated the British in 1783, Pennsylvania's key role in the war had earned it the nickname Keystone.

**Valley Forge**

The wedge-shaped keystone at the top of an arch holds the arch together. Pennsylvania helped hold the colonies together during the revolution.

In 1787 representatives from the former British colonies came to Philadelphia to write their new nation's **constitution,** or laws. Pennsylvania was the second state to ratify, or approve, the Constitution of the United States of America.

Pennsylvania takes pride in its motto—"Virtue, Liberty, and Independence"—which is printed on the state flag.

Pennsylvania was the richest state in the country. Farmers there grew grain for milling into flour. Miners in northeastern Pennsylvania dug coal, while workers in Scranton and other growing cities made more iron than in any other state in the Union.

With 42,000 people in 1790, Philadelphia was the nation's largest city. The port of Philadelphia was also the first stop for many **immigrants,** or settlers from other countries.

Some immigrants found jobs in textile and flour mills along Philadelphia's rivers. Immigrants looking for less crowded land generally headed to Pittsburgh, a gateway to the American frontier. Pioneers stocked up on supplies at Pittsburgh's busy stores and then traveled west by wagon or river barge.

**The Conestoga wagon, invented in Pennsylvania in the 1790s, was popular with settlers traveling west.**

Crossing the Allegheny Mountains in the mid-1800s was quite an adventure. Canal-boat passengers going west to Johnstown were loaded—boat and all—onto railcars that took them over the steepest peaks.

Settlers and other travelers often found it hard to get from one part of the state to another because of the lack of roads. Merchants and manufacturers also wished for easier routes across the state, especially over the steep mountains of central Pennsylvania.

In the early 1800s, miles of roads and many new bridges were built in the state. Canals linked Philadelphia and Pittsburgh by 1834. Travel between eastern and western Pennsylvania was made even easier when railroads crossed the mountains in the 1850s.

31

Philadelphia's William Still, a conductor on the Underground Railroad, helped bring many slaves to freedom.

A different kind of railroad, called the **Underground Railroad,** brought a number of African Americans to the Keystone State from the early- to mid-1800s. This railroad had no cars or tracks. Instead it was the name for a secret system of routes taking slaves from the South to freedom in the North.

In towns like Pine Forge, Grove City, and Lewisburg, "conductors" worked on Pennsylvania's Underground Railroad. These volunteers hid, fed, and helped find safe passage for hundreds of slaves escaping to freedom.

Slavery was dividing the country. Owning people was illegal in Pennsylvania and other Northern states. Many Pennsylvanians thought slavery was wrong.

In 1860 Southern states began withdrawing from the Union to form the Confederacy, a separate nation where slavery was legal. By 1861 tensions between the Confederacy and the Union led to war.

Pennsylvania stood behind the Union throughout the Civil War. Ironworkers supplied the Union army with guns and ammunition. Philadelphia's bankers loaned the Union money to fight the war. Textile workers wove cloth for uniforms. And Pennsylvanians from all parts of the state lost their lives in battle.

**Union soldier**

Modern-day "soldiers" put on costumes and reenact the Battle of Gettysburg each year.

The Battle of Gettysburg, in south central Pennsylvania, was the most deadly battle waged in the state. Between the first and third of July 1863, more than 50,000 men were wounded or killed in what was called the Most Terrible Struggle of the War.

The Confederate army lost as many as 28,000 men at Gettysburg. With such heavy losses, the Confederates no longer had enough soldiers to lead major attacks. For the Union, Gettysburg was the turning point in the war. By 1865 the Confederacy had been defeated.

In the 1890s, workers at the Homestead steelworks near Pittsburgh produced 25,000 tons (22,500 metric tons) of steel each month.

After the war, Pennsylvanians set about meeting the needs of the nation. High-quality coal was discovered in western Pennsylvania, and miners found jobs digging it out. Mills sprang up in Pittsburgh, using coal power to make steel for railroad ties, machinery, and bridge supports. By the late 1800s, Pennsylvania was leading the country in manufacturing and mining.

Pittsburgh and other cities in Pennsylvania had so many jobs that immigrants came there by the thousands. Leaving homes in Hungary, Poland, Russia, Ukraine, and other parts of Europe, most immigrants worked in Pennsylvania's mines, mills, and factories.

# Water, Water, Everywhere

Johnstown, in southwestern Pennsylvania, was like many of the state's growing cities in the late 1800s. Workers crowded into Johnstown, and factories seemed to have jobs for everyone. But while the city grew, a terrible danger lay in the mountains nearby.

Johnstown is in a deep valley at the meeting place of the Little Conemaugh River and Stony Creek. People there were used to flooding. They were also used to joking about the old South Fork Dam at a mountain lake high above the city. "Well, this is the day the old dam is going to break," people would joke on rainy days.

On May 31, 1889, the dam did break. Water streaming through the broken dam hit Johnstown so fast that it picked up trees and train cars and tossed them in the air. Over 2,000 men, women, and children died in the flood and in a great fire that raged in the wreckage of houses trapped against a bridge. In about 10 minutes, nearly all of Johnstown was destroyed or under water.

When it was all over, the people of Johnstown were stunned. They rebuilt their city and faced high water and floods again in later years. But none has ever matched the power and destruction of the 1889 Johnstown Flood.

**Breaker boys worked long hours in the breaker—an unheated room outside a coal mine—picking shale out of heaps of coal.**

Life for Pennsylvania's workers in the late 1800s wasn't easy, especially for young people. When families couldn't make ends meet, children went out to work—often for as many as 60 hours per week.

At that time, it was against the law for anyone under the age of 12 to have a job in the Keystone State. But more children worked in Pennsylvania than in any other state in the Union.

Many young Pennsylvanians continued to work long hours until the 1930s, when jobs were hard for anyone—young or old—to find. This period of hard times, from 1929 to about 1939, was called the Great Depression. During the depression, businesses and banks closed, and people lost their jobs. Even people who had jobs found it difficult to get by as wages fell.

The depression ended when the country entered the Second World War in 1941. During the war, more than one million Pennsylvanians served in the armed forces. Many jobs were created, as Pennsylvanians made warships, uniforms, and chocolate bars for soldiers.

**Unemployed men gather in a Philadelphia park during the Great Depression.**

**Cars line up to drive the first stretch of the Pennsylvania Turnpike on opening weekend in 1940.**

When the war ended in 1945, many former soldiers were hired to work in Pennsylvania's factories. New highways such as the Pennsylvania Turnpike made it easier to send goods to other states.

In the last 50 years, Pennsylvania has been a state of problems and promise. In 1979 a serious accident occurred at Three Mile Island, near Harrisburg. Three Mile Island was a plant that used **nuclear power** to create electricity.

During the accident, a small amount of dangerous **radioactive** gas escaped. The power plant was contaminated and had to be shut down for cleanup.

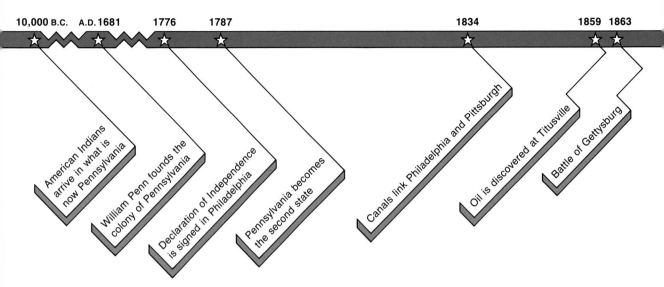

10,000 B.C.  A.D. 1681  1776  1787  1834  1859  1863

American Indians arrive in what is now Pennsylvania

William Penn founds the colony of Pennsylvania

Declaration of Independence is signed in Philadelphia

Pennsylvania becomes the second state

Canals link Philadelphia and Pittsburgh

Oil is discovered at Titusville

Battle of Gettysburg

While such problems grab headlines in newspapers across the country, Pennsylvanians take pride in the many promising changes in their state. For example, Pittsburgh, once called Smoky City because of pollution, is now ranked one of the best places to live in the country. With its clean air and water, Pittsburgh shows the promise of Pennsylvania's future.

**Pittsburgh**
*(facing page)*

40

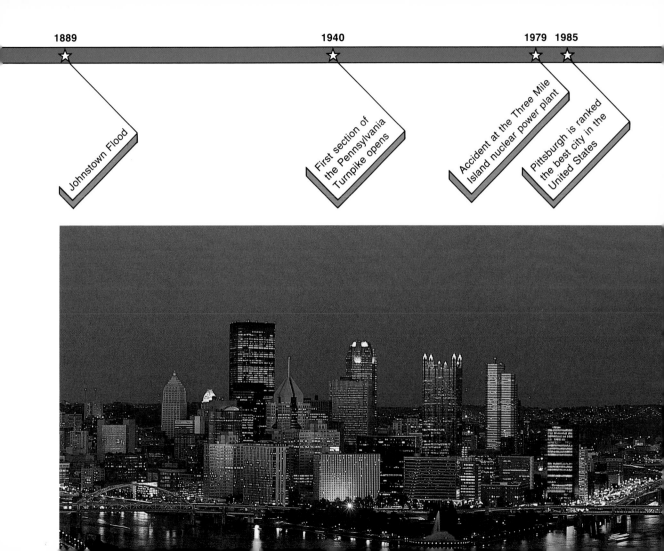

1889
Johnstown Flood

1940
First section of the Pennsylvania Turnpike opens

1979
Accident at the Three Mile Island nuclear power plant

1985
Pittsburgh is ranked the best city in the United States

**Pennsylvania offers the excitement of big cities such as Allentown** *(above)* **and the peace and quiet of small towns** *(left).*

# Living and Working in Pennsylvania

Pittsburgh in the west and Philadelphia in the east are the two biggest cities in the Keystone State, but there's more than just a turnpike in between. Fascinating places and people can be found in every corner of the state.

Pennsylvania's population is big and diverse. With nearly 12 million people, the state has the fifth largest population in the country.

Native Americans were once the only people in the area. Nowadays, 88 percent of Pennsylvanians are white people of European backgrounds.

A Mennonite girl gives a welcoming smile.

43

**William Penn's statue atop city hall watches over bustling downtown Philadelphia.**

African Americans make up about 9 percent of the state's population. Smaller numbers of Pennsylvanians are **Latinos** (people with Latin American roots), Asian Americans, and Native Americans.

Philadelphia is the largest city in the state. It is home to people of many different ethnic backgrounds. With more than 1.5 million residents, Philadelphia easily tops Pittsburgh, which has about 370,000 people. Other big cities in Pennsylvania include Erie, Allentown, and Scranton.

About 21 percent of working Pennsylvanians are employed in manufacturing. Many of the biggest steel companies in the country are located in the Keystone State, but steel isn't the only thing Pennsylvanians produce.

At food-processing companies such as H. J. Heinz in Pittsburgh, people make everything from ketchup to baby food. Candy makers at the world's largest chocolate factory in Hershey, Pennsylvania, produce tons of chocolate bars.

In Philadelphia at the University of Pennsylvania, researchers built the first general-purpose computer in 1946. Nowadays, workers in the Philadelphia area turn out computers and information systems.

**With the world's largest chocolate factory and with street lamps shaped like chocolate kisses, Hershey, Pennsylvania, is a chocolate-lover's dream.**

45

**Dairy farming is a small but important part of the Keystone State's economy.**

Though many Native Americans and early European settlers farmed the land, nowadays only 2 percent of Pennsylvanians work in agriculture. The state's farmers keep busy raising greenhouse vegetables, corn, and dairy cattle.

With its rich deposits of coal, Pennsylvania has had a long history of mining. Since the 1950s, however, many of Pennsylvania's coal mines have shut down, as other fuels have become more popular. Now only 1 percent of the state's workers are miners.

Most people in Pennsylvania have service jobs, in which they work helping others. Service workers run government offices in Harrisburg, the state capital. They staff hospitals and meet the needs of tourists throughout the state.

**A worker** *(above left)* **drills a hole for explosives at a coal mine in west central Pennsylvania. In Harrisburg, government employees work in offices in the capitol building** *(above)*.

String-band members, dressed-up dancers, and many more Philadelphians take part in the annual Mummers' Parade.

It's easy to see why tourists visit Pennsylvania when you take a look at what's going on in the Keystone State. On New Year's Day, Philadelphians take to the streets in the Mummers' Parade.

The parade's roots combine German and African American traditions of greeting the new year.

Mummers entertain the crowds with their music, fancy dancing, and big, bright costumes.

In Pittsburgh people celebrate the arts with the Three Rivers Arts Festival each June. At the Three Rivers Regatta in August, boat parades and waterskiing events fill the city's rivers.

**Whether little league** (*left*) **or big league** (*right*), **sports are popular in the Keystone State.**

Big cities aren't the only places to find fun in the Keystone State. Each August the small town of Williamsport in north central Pennsylvania is taken over by baseball lovers young and old. Teams from around the country play there in the Little League World Series.

Fans of professional sports have a lot to choose from in Pennsylvania. The Phillies play baseball in Philadelphia, while the Pirates hit runs for the home crowd in Pittsburgh. The state also has professional basketball, hockey, and football teams.

For people who prefer facts to footballs, Pennsylvania offers a taste of the past at historic sites across the state. Philadelphia's Independence National Historical Park has more history per square foot than almost any other spot in the nation. In just a few downtown blocks, you can visit Independence Hall, see the famous Liberty Bell, and stand at the site of Benjamin Franklin's house.

Back in the 1700s, silversmith Philip Syng lived on Elfreth's Alley, now Philadelphia's oldest street. Syng made the inkwell used to sign the Declaration of Independence and the U.S. Constitution.

# A Few

## Firsts

A longtime Philadelphian and a signer of the Declaration of Independence, Benjamin Franklin was also a great inventor. He created a metal rod that stopped lightning bolts from hitting buildings and starting fires. Franklin's invention of bifocal glasses still helps people see both close up and far away. And versions of the cast-iron Franklin stove, which he first built in 1744, have warmed homes in Pennsylvania and across the country ever since.

**Amish boys in Lancaster County head to school.**

Lancaster County, west of Philadelphia, sometimes looks like a history museum. That's because the area's Amish and Mennonite farmers follow centuries-old traditions. Some still speak the language of their German and Swiss ancestors. For religious reasons, many Amish and some Mennonites choose to live in homes without electricity and to ride in horse-drawn buggies.

**Philadelphia Zoo**

Although Pennsylvania is full of traditions and history, it's also packed with new places and ideas. At Pittsburgh's Carnegie science museum, you can walk through a huge model of the human digestive system. The Futures Center at Philadelphia's Franklin Institute will give you a preview of life in the next century. With attractions old and new, the Keystone State is a great place to visit. And, as Pennsylvanians will tell you, it's not a bad place to live either.

**Sesame Place, a theme park in Langhorne, Pennsylvania, packs a lot of fun into a small space.**

**Rainfall in the Keystone State helps flowers grow, but it also contains high levels of acid.**

54

# Protecting the Environment

Drip, drip, drip. As rain falls each spring, it helps crops grow and flows into streams all over Pennsylvania. But that rain can also hold hidden dangers.

**Acid rain** refers to rain or other precipitation that is high in acid. Pennsylvania has some of the most acidic rain, snow, sleet, and fog in the country. Acid rain kills fish in lakes in the state's Pocono Mountains. It can cause metals in storage-tank linings to seep into drinking water. And it is slowly eating away at bronze and stone monuments at Gettysburg National Military Park and elsewhere.

How can rain that looks clean and pure be bad? Scientists have known for a long time that rain falling downwind from industrial areas often contains a lot of acid. They use the **pH** scale to measure how much acid is present. On the pH scale, the lower the number, the higher the level of acid.

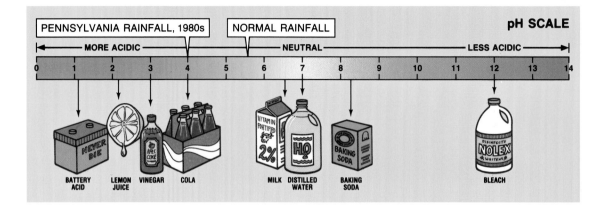

PENNSYLVANIA RAINFALL, 1980s

NORMAL RAINFALL

MORE ACIDIC — NEUTRAL — LESS ACIDIC

0  1  2  3  4  5  6  7  8  9  10  11  12  13  14

BATTERY ACID — LEMON JUICE — VINEGAR — COLA — MILK — DISTILLED WATER — BAKING SODA — BLEACH

Unpolluted rain, for example, contains very little acid and has a pH of about 5.6. During the 1980s, rainfall in Pennsylvania had an average pH of about 4.0, which is about as acidic as cola.

Acid rain is caused when high levels of sulfur dioxide and nitrogen oxide gather in the air. These chemicals come from coal-burning power plants and from car exhaust.

Power plants in the state burn Pennsylvania coal to create electricity. Much of the coal mined in Pennsylvania is high in sulfur. When burned, this coal sends clouds of sulfur dioxide into the atmosphere. Exhaust from cars and trucks contains nitrogen oxide, which passes into the air. These chemicals can return to the ground as acid precipitation.

**Pennsylvania's coal-burning power plants** *(above)* **send nearly 1.5 million tons (1.35 million metric tons) of sulfur dioxide into the air each year. When such chemicals form acid rain, they can pollute mountain streams** *(upper right).*

Pennsylvanians are working to offset damage from acid rain. For example, the state regularly waits to stock trout streams until after spring snows melt. Snow can have especially high levels of acid. Once acidic snowmelts have run through streams, the water is safer for young fish.

Many pieces of sculpture at Philadelphia's Fairmount Park have been covered with a layer of wax to protect against damage from acid rain.

At Gettysburg, monuments are carefully cleaned and covered with a layer of protective wax. Sculptures in Philadelphia's Fairmount Park have also been protected in this way.

Many Pennsylvanians who drink rainwater stored in tanks are testing their water more often. The acids in acid rain can eat away at metal linings in water tanks and pollute the water. Older tanks are being replaced.

But Pennsylvanians are also working to stop acid rain at its source. The state has set tough standards for lowering the amount of sulfur dioxide and nitrogen oxide that power plants and factories can put out. National laws now call for less-polluting cars and trucks and set goals for cleaner air across the country.

Smokestacks at many coal-burning plants in Pennsylvania have been fitted with scrubbers to filter out sulfur dioxide. Plants are also switching to low-sulfur coal.

# Keeping an Eye on

ACID RAIN

Each year, Pennsylvania receives some of the most acidic rainfall in the country. But scientists have discovered that acid rain causes less damage in Pennsylvania than in some other states.

Why? Geologists have the answer. Most of Pennsylvania's soil and rocks are naturally low in acid. They can absorb the acid in acid rain without great harm. But not all areas in Pennsylvania have this natural ability. In the Pocono Mountains, for example, the thin, rocky soil cannot absorb much acid. Many lakes and streams in the Poconos have been damaged or are in danger of future damage from acid rain.

To keep an eye on conditions in the Poconos and throughout the state, Pennsylvania has set up monitoring stations. Samples of rain and other precipitation taken at these stations are tested for their pH level and for sulfur dioxide and nitrogen oxide. By keeping an eye on acid levels, scientists in Pennsylvania hope to keep on top of the dangers of acid rain.

Reducing the causes of acid rain has created some new problems. When scrubbers at power plants filter out sulfur dioxide, for example, they leave behind tons of sludge. Scrubber sludge is piling up fast in the state's landfills. Most low-sulfur coal comes from out of state, so switching from coal mined in the state may mean fewer jobs for Pennsylvania's coal miners.

Despite these setbacks, Pennsylvania's efforts are paying off. The amount of sulfur dioxide produced in Pennsylvania went down by 23 percent between 1980 and 1985, and the trend continues. Nitrogen oxide levels are also decreasing. By tackling this threat to the environment head-on, Pennsylvania is now a keystone state in its efforts to take the acid out of acid rain.

**Pennsylvania's efforts to reduce acid rain are working in the Pocono Mountains, where acid levels in lakes** *(facing page)* **and streams** *(above)* **are declining.**

# Pennsylvania's Famous People

◄ MICHAEL KEATON

## ACTORS & ENTERTAINERS

**Bill Cosby** (born 1937) was television's most popular dad during the 1980s in his role as Dr. Heathcliff Huxtable on "The Cosby Show." The Philadelphia native is also a well-known writer, comedian, and television producer.

**Michael Keaton** (born 1951) grew up in Forest Grove, near Pittsburgh. Keaton turned to acting—and won the starring role in the movie *Batman*—after driving a cab and an ice-cream truck for several years.

**Patti LaBelle** (born 1944), star of television's "Out All Night," was born in Philadelphia. She started her career as a singer with the group Patti LaBelle and the Blue Bells. Since the 1960s, LaBelle has had hit singles such as "Lady Marmalade."

BILL COSBY ►

▼ FRED ROGERS

▲ PATTI LABELLE

**Fred Rogers** (born 1928) of Latrobe, Pennsylvania, has been asking children "Won't you be my neighbor?" since the 1950s. Host of television's "Mister Rogers' Neighborhood," Rogers is famous for saying, "There's only one person in the world like you, and I like you just the way you are."

## ARTISTS

**Alexander Calder** (1898–1976) was born in Lawnton, Pennsylvania, and studied engineering before becoming a sculptor. Calder is famous for his mobiles—sculptures that hang by wires and move with currents of air.

62

◀ MARY CASSATT

HENRY O. ▶
TANNER

**Mary Cassatt** (1844–1926) was a native of Allegheny City, Pennsylvania, but grew up in Europe. Impressed by the paintings she saw there, Cassatt became an artist.

**Henry O. Tanner** (1859–1937), of Pittsburgh, studied art in Philadelphia but left for Europe to continue his education and to avoid racism against African Americans. He is best known for his paintings of southern blacks and scenes from the Bible.

## ATHLETES

**Reggie Jackson** (born 1946) was a track, baseball, and football star at his Wyncote, Pennsylvania, high school. Jackson later concentrated on baseball and led the Oakland Athletics to three World Series victories in the 1970s.

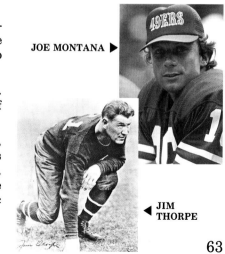

JOE MONTANA ▶

◀ JIM THORPE

**Joe Montana** (born 1956) grew up in Monongahela, Pennsylvania. A football player, Montana earned the nickname the Comeback Quarterback during his years with the San Francisco 49ers.

**Arnold Palmer** (born 1929) is a Latrobe, Pennsylvania, native. Palmer is the first golfer in history to win the Masters Golf Tournament four times.

**Jim Thorpe** (1886–1953), a Sauk and Fox Native American, studied at the Indian school in Carlisle, Pennsylvania. Thorpe's ability on the football field drew large crowds to Carlisle games, but he is best known for winning gold medals in both the decathlon and pentathlon—two tests of all-around athletic ability—at the 1912 Olympics.

▲ WILLIAM WHIPPER

◀ ANDREW CARNEGIE

## BUSINESS LEADERS

**Andrew Carnegie** (1835–1919) came to Allegheny, Pennsylvania, from Scotland. Carnegie first worked changing spools of thread in a textile mill. By the end of his career, he ran a steelmaking empire and was one of the richest men in the world.

**William Whipper** (1805–1885), the son of a white businessman and a black servant, built a fortune in the lumber trade in Lancaster County. Whipper gave much of his time and money to ending slavery.

## JOURNALISTS

**Nellie Bly** (1867–1922) was born in Cochrane Mills, Pennsylvania. Forced to support her family as a young woman, she became a newspaper reporter. Bly became famous when she disguised herself as a disturbed woman and then wrote about her experiences in a mental hospital.

**Ida Minerva Tarbell** (1857–1944) grew up in Titusville, Pennsylvania, during the area's oil boom. Tarbell worked as a journalist, exposing an oil company's dishonest business deals.

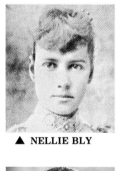

▲ NELLIE BLY

▲ IDA MINERVA TARBELL

◀ MARIAN ANDERSON

## SINGERS

**Marian Anderson** (1897–1993) began her singing career at the age of six in Philadelphia's Union Baptist church choir. She grew up to be one of the greatest singers of her time, performing in concert and in opera.

64

Chubby Checker (born 1941) was born Ernest Evans in Philadelphia. While working as a chicken plucker in a poultry shop, he entertained customers so much that the store's owner introduced him to a record producer. Using the name Chubby Checker, he sang and danced on television in the 1960s.

◀ CHUBBY CHECKER

Nathan Morris (born 1970), Michael McCary (born 1971), Shawn Stockman (born 1971), and Wanya Morris (born 1973) are all part of Boyz II Men. The Boyz have been harmonizing in Philadelphia since 1991 with their first album, *Cooleyhighharmony*.

JERRY SPINELLI ▶

BOYZ II MEN ▶

## WRITERS

Lloyd Alexander (born 1924) grew up in West Philadelphia, where he bought a copy of *King Arthur and His Knights* at a local bookshop. From the legends and heroic tales he read as a child, Alexander has created fantasy heroes in over 20 books for children.

Jerry Spinelli (born 1941) is a native of Norristown, Pennsylvania. Spinelli began writing while still in high school. His novels for young readers include *Maniac Magee, Fourth Grade Rats,* and *There's a Girl in My Hammerlock.*

◀ AUGUST WILSON

August Wilson (born 1945) is a Pulitzer prize-winning playwright. In *Fences* and other works, Wilson draws on his experiences growing up African American in Pittsburgh.

65

# Facts-at-a-Glance

**Nicknames:** Keystone State, Quaker State
**Song:** none
**Motto:** Virtue, Liberty, and Independence
**Flower:** mountain laurel
**Tree:** hemlock
**Bird:** ruffed grouse

**Population:** 11,881,643*
**Rank in population, nationwide:** 5th
**Area:** 46,058 sq mi (119,090 sq km)
**Rank in area, nationwide:** 33rd
**Date and ranking of statehood:**
  December 12, 1787, the 2nd state
**Capital:** Harrisburg (52,376*)
**Major cities (and populations*):**
  Philadelphia (1,585,577), Pittsburgh (369,879),
  Erie (108,718), Allentown (105,090),
  Scranton (81,805)
**U.S. senators:** 2
**U.S. representatives:** 19
**Electoral votes:** 21

**Places to visit:** Pennsylvania Dutch country in southeastern Pennsylvania, Independence Hall and the Liberty Bell in Philadelphia, Hawk Mountain Bird Sanctuary in the Kittatinny Mountains, French Azilum near Towanda, Fallingwater near Mill Run, Hershey Chocolate World in Hershey

**Annual events:** Mummers' Parade in Philadelphia (Jan.), Chocolate Festival in Hershey (Feb.), Little League Baseball World Series in Williamsport (Aug.), Bean Soup Festival in McClure (Sept.), Kwanzaa celebration in Philadelphia (Dec.–Jan.)

*1990 Census

66

**Average January temperature:** 27° F (−3° C)   **Average July temperature:** 71° F (22° C)

**Natural resources:** fertile soil, coal, natural gas, limestone, water, oil, sand, gravel, slate

**Agricultural products:** milk and dairy products, greenhouse vegetables, hay, beef, eggs, corn

**Manufactured goods:** electrical equipment, computers, steel, aluminum, paper, prescription drugs, petroleum products, baby foods, soups, potato chips

ENDANGERED SPECIES
**Mammals**—least shrew, Indiana bat, Delmarva fox squirrel
**Birds**—peregrine falcon, osprey, short-eared owl, bald eagle
**Amphibians and reptiles**—bog turtle, coastal plain leopard frog, New Jersey chorus frog
**Fish**—longnose sucker, gravel chub, eastern sand darter, northern brook lamprey
**Plants**—spreading globe-flower, Jacob's ladder

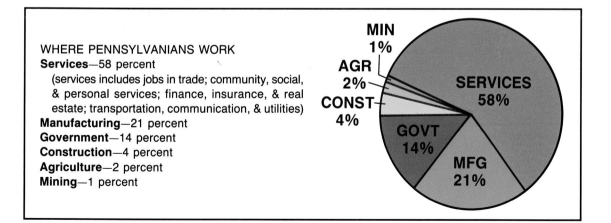

WHERE PENNSYLVANIANS WORK
**Services**—58 percent
(services includes jobs in trade; community, social, & personal services; finance, insurance, & real estate; transportation, communication, & utilities)
**Manufacturing**—21 percent
**Government**—14 percent
**Construction**—4 percent
**Agriculture**—2 percent
**Mining**—1 percent

MIN 1%
AGR 2%
CONST 4%
SERVICES 58%
GOVT 14%
MFG 21%

**acid rain** Any precipitation which is high in acid. Acid rain occurs when rain or other precipitation passes through an atmosphere polluted with sulfur dioxide and nitrogen oxide.

**colony** A territory ruled by a country some distance away.

**constitution** The system of basic laws or rules of a government, society, or organization. The document in which these laws or rules are written.

**Great Lakes** A chain of five lakes in Canada and the northern United States. They are Lakes Superior, Michigan, Huron, Erie, and Ontario.

**immigrant** A person who moves to a foreign country and settles there.

**Latino** A person living in the United

States who either came from or has ancestors from Latin America.

**nuclear power** A way of producing energy and electricity using atoms, the tiny building blocks of the universe.

**pH** A measure of the level of acid in a substance.

**precipitation** Rain, snow, and other forms of moisture that fall to earth.

**radioactive** Giving off rays of energy called radiation, which happens when atoms of certain elements change to other elements.

**turnpike** A highway on which a toll, or fee, is collected from drivers at various points along the route.

**Underground Railroad** A system of escape routes that helped slaves get from the South to the North or Canada, where they would be free.

**Thousands visit Fallingwater, a house built over a running stream near Mill Run, Pennsylvania, each year.**

# Index ━━━━▶

Acid rain, 54–61
African Americans, 32, 44, 48
Agriculture, 12–13, 17, 18, 19, 21, 22, 28, 30, 46, 52, 55
Allegheny National Forest, 15, 16
Allentown, 42, 44
Animals, 6, 16–17, 18, 21
Appalachian Plateau, 10, 12, 16
Appalachian Ridge, 12
Atlantic Coastal Plain, 14

Charles II, king of Britain, 22
Chocolate, 38, 45
Cities and towns, 6, 12, 32, 45, 49, 52, 53. *See also* Allentown; Erie; Gettysburg; Harrisburg; Hershey; Johnstown; Philadelphia; Pittsburgh; Scranton
Climate, 6, 17, 54–55
Coal, 12, 30, 35, 37, 46, 47, 56, 57, 58, 60
Conestoga wagon, 30
Confederacy, 33–34
Constitution of the United States of America, 26, 29, 50
Continental Congresses, 26–27

Declaration of Independence, 26, 27, 50, 51
Delaware River and Delaware River valley, 14, 18, 20, 21, 22

Economy, 30, 31, 35, 37–39, 45–47, 60
Energy sources, 12, 35, 39, 56, 57, 58, 60. *See also* Coal
Environment, 40, 54–61
Erie, 14, 44
Erie Lowland, 14
Ethnic makeup, 20–21, 22, 30, 35, 43–44, 48, 52. *See also* Pennsylvania Dutch

Festivals, 48, 53
Fish and fishing, 18–19, 55, 57
Flag, 29
Forests, 15, 16
Fox, George, 20
France, 24
Franklin, Benjamin, 50–51
Friends. *See* Society of Friends

Germany, 7, 13, 22, 48, 52
Gettysburg, 34, 55, 58
Great Britain, 20, 22, 24, 25–29
Great Valley, 12

Harrisburg, 15, 39, 47
Health and diseases, 24, 28
Hershey, 45

Hicks, Edward, 23
History, 18–41; ancient, 10, 18–19; colonial, 21–26; 1800s, 31–37; Great Depression, 38; independence, 26–29; 1900s, 38–41; settlers, 20–23, 24, 30–31; 1700s, 24–30; 1600s, 16, 20–23; statehood, 29; timeline, 40–41
Hudson, Henry, 20
Hunting, 18–19, 21, 24

Independence Hall, 26, 27, 50
Indians, 18–19, 20–21, 22, 43, 44, 46; Lenape (Delawares), 18–19, 20, 23, 24; Monongahela, 18–19; Susquehannocks, 18–19
Inventions, 7, 51
Iron and steel, 30, 33, 35, 45

Jobs, 30, 33, 35, 36, 37–39, 45–47, 60
Johnstown, 12, 31, 36

Lakes, 14–15, 55, 59, 60–61
Liberty Bell, 27, 50
Little League (baseball) World Series, 49

Manufacturing and industries, 28, 30, 31, 33, 35, 36, 38–39, 45, 58. *See also* Iron and steel

Military, 21, 26–28, 33–34, 38–39

Mining, 30, 35, 46, 47, 60. *See also* Coal

Mountains, 8, 10, 12, 17, 31, 36. *See also* Pocono Mountains

Native Americans. *See* Indians

Penn, William, 20, 22–24, 44

Pennsylvania: boundaries and location, 9, 10, 15; ethnic makeup, 20–21, 22, 30, 35, 43–44, 48, 52; Facts-at-a-Glance, 66–67; Famous People, 62–65; flag of, 29; maps and charts, 11, 56; nicknames, 28, 40; origin of name, 22; population, 22, 30, 43, 44; statehood, 29

Pennsylvania Dutch, 7, 13, 22, 52

Pennsylvania Turnpike and highways, 8–9, 17, 31, 39

Philadelphia, 14, 26, 27, 28, 29, 30, 31, 32, 33, 38, 43, 44, 45, 48, 49, 50, 51, 52, 53, 58

Piedmont region, 13

Pittsburgh, 7, 15, 30, 31, 35, 40–41, 43, 44, 45, 48, 49, 53

Plants, 17

Pocono Mountains, 10, 55, 59, 60–61

Pollution, 40, 54–61

Population, 22, 30, 43, 44

Quakers. *See* Society of Friends

Railroads, 7, 12, 31, 35

Religion, 20, 22, 52. *See also* Society of Friends

Rivers and waterways, 15, 18, 30, 36, 48, 55, 57, 59, 60. *See also* Delaware River and Delaware River valley

Scranton, 30, 44

Slavery, 32–33

Society of Friends, 20, 22–23

Sports and recreation, 10, 15, 48–53

Still, William, 32

Switzerland, 7, 13, 22, 52

Syng, Philip, 50

Tamanend, 24

Three Mile Island, 39

Tourism, 47, 48, 53

Transportation, 14, 15, 17, 30–31. *See also* Pennsylvania Turnpike and highways; Railroads

Underground Railroad, 32

United States of America (Union), 29, 33–34

Valley Forge, 28

Wars and battles, 24–25, 26–29, 33–34, 38

Washington, George, 27–28

**Acknowledgments:**

Maryland Cartographics, Inc., pp. 2, 11; Mae Scanlan, pp. 2–3, 9, 12, 28, 47 (right), 61; Jack Lindstrom, p. 6; Michael Medford, p. 7; Endless Mountains Visitors Bureau, p. 8; © Sally Weigand, pp. 10, 53 (top left), 57 (upper right), 58, 60; Chester County Tourist Bureau, pp. 13, 18; Erie Area Chamber of Commerce, pp. 14, 54 (bottom); PA Dutch Convention & Visitors Bureau, pp. 15, 42 (bottom); Sylvia Schlender, p. 16 (left); Jerry Hennen, pp. 16 (inset), 17; Library Company of Philadelphia, pp. 19, 21; Library of Congress, pp. 22, 36, 37, 64 (upper left); Mr. & Mrs. Meyer P. Potamkin, p. 23; IPS, pp. 25, 32, 64 (center left and right); Thomas P. Benincas, Jr., pp. 26, 27, 44; Print & Picture Collection, Free Library of Philadelphia, p. 30; MG–219 Commercial Museum Collection, PA State Archives, p. 31; Lehigh County Historical Society, p. 33; Paul Witt, p. 34; California Museum of Photography, Keystone-Mast Collection, U. of CA Riverside, p. 35; Urban Archives, Temple Univ., Philadelphia, PA, p. 38; PA Turnpike Commission, p. 39; John R. Patton, pp. 41, 46, 47 (top left), 52, 57 (left); Lehigh Valley Convention & Visitors Bureau, p. 42 (top); Betty Groskin, p. 43; Harrisburg-Hershey-Carlisle Tourism & Convention Bureau, p. 45 (right); Hershey Entertainment & Resort Co., p. 45 (top left); Colin P. Varga, pp. 48, 51; Little League Baseball, p. 49 (left); Philadelphia Convention and Visitors Bureau, p. 49 (right); James Blank / Root Resources, p. 50; Bucks County Tourist Comm., p. 53 (right); PA Dept. of Environmental Resources, pp. 54 (inset), 59 (photo by Paul Zeph); Hollywood Book & Poster, pp. 62 (all), 65 (top); *Portrait of the Artist* (detail), Metropolitan Museum of Art, Bequest of Edith H. Proskauer, 1975, p. 63 (top); Henry Ossawa Tanner Papers (detail), Archives of American Art, Smithsonian Institution, p. 63 (center left); Football Hall of Fame, p. 63 (bottom); San Francisco 49ers, p. 63 (center right); NY State Historical Association, Cooperstown, p. 64 (top); Station KSTP, Minneapolis, p. 64 (bottom); Motown Records, p. 65 (center right); © M. Elaine Adams / Ray Lincoln Literary Agency, p. 65 (center left); Univ. of Pittsburgh, p. 65 (bottom left); Jean Matheny, p. 66; © Shmuel Thaler, pp. 69, 71.